by **Stuart Schwartz and Craig Conley**

Consultant:
Karen Wagner
Manager
Mankato WorkForce Center

CAPSTONE
HIGH/LOW BOOKS
an imprint of Capstone Press
Mankato, Minnesota

Capstone High/Low Books are published by Capstone Press
818 North Willow Street, Mankato, Minnesota 56001
http://www.capstone-press.com

Library of Congress Cataloging-in-Publication Data
Schwartz, Stuart, 1945–
    Writing a resumé/by Stuart Schwartz and Craig Conley.
    p. cm.—(Looking at work)
    Includes bibliographical references and index.
    Summary: Examines the purpose of a resume, the basics and style, the different
kinds, how to plan, write, and strengthen one, and how to keep it up-to-date.
    ISBN 0-7368-0181-2
    1. Resumés (Employment)—Juvenile literature. [1. Resumés (Employment)]
I. Conley, Craig, 1965–. II. Title. III. Series: Schwartz, Stuart, 1945–   Looking
at work.
HF5392.S38 1999
808'.06665—dc21   98-31851
                                                                                  CIP
                                                                                   AC

Editorial Credits

Carrie Braulick, editor; Steve Christensen, cover designer; Kimberly Danger and
    Sheri Gosewisch, photo researchers

Photo Credits

David F. Clobes, 4, 8, 12, 14, 26
Diane Meyer, 10
Photophile, 22
Uniphoto, cover
Visuals Unlimited/Warren Stone, 24

Table of Contents

Chapter 1

Purpose of a Resumé

Job seekers write resumés to help them get jobs. Resumés tell employers about job seekers' experiences, education, and skills. Employers review resumés. They may choose to meet with certain job seekers. These meetings are called job interviews.

Resumés help employers decide which job seekers will best fit their needs. Many employers look for certain information on resumés. For example, some jobs require workers who speak and write well. Employers look for resumés that show job seekers have these skills.

Employers like resumés that are neat and well organized. Many employers need to see information quickly. Well-written resumés help them to do this.

Resumés help employers decide which job seekers to interview.

Terry Newton
436 Wells Road
Warren, RI 02885
(000) 000-0000

OBJECTIVE   To work as a computer sales representative

WORK   Sales Representative, Computers Plus,
EXPERIENCE   Pawtucket, RI, 1994-1998
• sold computer equipment
• assisted customers

Computer Lab Assistant, Brown
University, Providence, RI, 1993-1997
• assisted students with computer problems
• produced worksheets and handbooks to
  help students use computer programs

EDUCATION   Brown University, Providence, RI
• Bachelor of Science degree in computer
  science, May 1997
• minor: psychology

ACTIVITIES   • received certificate for selling the most
& AWARDS   software at Computers Plus, 1997
• president, Student Marketing Association,
  Brown University, 1994-1996
• member, Computer Technology Club,
  Brown University, 1994

References available upon request.

Chapter 2

Resumé Basics

Resumés provide basic information to employers. They list facts about job seekers. For example, they include job seekers' names, addresses, and phone numbers. This information helps employers contact job seekers to arrange interviews.

Most job seekers explain their job goals on resumés. These goals are called objectives. Most objectives are one sentence long.

Many resumés include work experience. Job seekers list where they have worked. They tell what they did in past jobs. They may list how long they worked at each job.

Education sections also are included in resumés. Job seekers write about the training they received at schools in education sections.

Job seekers may list activities or awards on their resumés. This information helps prove that job seekers will be good workers.

Many job seekers include their objectives, work experience, and education on their resumés.

Chapter 3

Planning a Resumé

Job seekers plan their resumés. They carefully write and organize their resumés. Well-planned resumés help job seekers get better results.

Job seekers learn about jobs that interest them. They may learn about the education and skills required for certain jobs. This helps job seekers write objectives. It also helps them decide what information to include in their resumés.

Job seekers decide which information is most important to employers. They put that information first in their resumés. For example, some jobs require a strong education. People seeking these jobs list their education first.

Job seekers may want to review other resumés. This helps job seekers learn more about how to write their resumés. Schools may have sample resumés job seekers can review.

Job seekers carefully plan their resumés.

Chapter 4

Rules for Resumé Writing

Job seekers follow a few basic rules when they write resumés. This helps employers easily read resumés.

Employers prefer resumés that look professional. These resumés are typed or written on computers. Resumé paper size should be 8.5 by 11 inches (22 by 28 centimeters). Employers usually prefer one-page resumés.

Job seekers keep their resumés simple. They write short sentences. They only include the most important information in their resumés.

Job seekers follow the rules of the English language when they write resumés. They use correct grammar and punctuation. They also make sure all words are spelled correctly.

Most resumés are printed alike. They are printed in black ink. Many job seekers print or photocopy their resumés on white, ivory, off-white, or light gray paper.

Most resumés are printed on good quality, light-colored paper.

Chapter 5

Finishing a Resumé

Some employers look at many resumés before they arrange interviews. They may look at each resumé for only 20 to 30 seconds. This means job seekers must make their resumés stand out from others.

Many job seekers design their resumés to help employers see important points. Some job seekers use bold type for important information. For example, job seekers may put their names or section headings in bold type. Other job seekers underline certain parts of their resumés.

Most job seekers have other people check their resumés. Job seekers do this before they send their resumés to employers. People who help check resumés make sure the resumés do not have mistakes. They also make sure the resumés are neat and clear.

Most job seekers have other people check their resumés for mistakes.

Chapter 6

References

Employers sometimes ask job seekers for lists of references. References are people who know about job seekers' character and abilities. References share this information with employers.

Job seekers list about three references. Most job seekers choose people they know well as references. Teachers and past employers can be good references. Job seekers should ask permission from people before they list them as references.

Job seekers include the names, addresses, and telephone numbers of references on their lists. This helps employers contact references.

Most reference lists are printed on separate sheets of paper from resumés. Sometimes employers ask job seekers for reference lists at job interviews. Job seekers should always be ready to give employers their reference lists.

Employers sometimes ask for reference lists at job interviews.

Larry Weston
836 Nicollet Avenue
St. Paul, MN 55101
(000) 000-0000

Objective

To work as a manager of a large office

Work Experience

1994-1998

Business Assistant, Raymond Manufacturing, St. Cloud, MN
- Typed letters, reports, and other documents
- Arranged schedule for 75 employees
- Assisted in hiring office workers

1991-1994

Sales Department Assistant, Custom Building, Duluth, MN
- Reviewed sales reports
- Ordered supplies for department
- Supervised five sales clerks

1985-1991

Customer Service Worker, Great Solutions, Rochester, MN
- Organized customer files
- Handled customer telephone calls
- Helped produce company catalogs

Education

Riverland Technical College
Rochester, MN
Business Management, Associate in Applied Science Degree, May 1990

References available upon request.

Chapter 7

Chronological Resumés

Job seekers can write resumés in different styles. Each style has a purpose. Some job seekers use a chronological resumé style.

Chronological resumés list job seekers' work experience in order. They list the most recent work experience first. They include the dates job seekers worked at each job.

Chronological resumés also include other job information. They list names of companies. They list job seekers' job titles and duties. These resumés may include information about job seekers' accomplishments at work.

Some job seekers prefer chronological resumés. These job seekers may want jobs in areas that they have worked in for many years. They use chronological resumés to show their experience. Most job seekers who use this style have steady work histories. They also have recent experience in the job areas they seek.

Chronological resumés list work experience in order. These resumés begin with the most recent job.

Karen Wilcox
4367 Main Avenue
Raleigh, NC 27606
(000) 000-0000

Objective

To teach elementary school computer classes

Relevant Skills and Experience

Classroom Skills

Served as a student teacher in computer classes,
Seawell Elementary School, Chapel Hill, NC
Grade 6, May-Sept. 1998
- Taught children basic Internet and computer
  programming skills
- Taught children basic computer design skills

Leadership Skills

- Served as president of Future Leaders Club,
  North Carolina State University, 1995-1997
- Gained leadership skills as a lifeguard and
  swimming instructor, 1993-1998

Computer Skills

- Can create complex computer programs
- Have knowledge of most types of computer
  software and hardware

Education

- North Carolina State University, Raleigh, NC
  Bachelor of Arts in elementary education
  Minor: computer science

References available upon request.

Chapter 8

Functional Resumés

Functional resumés sometimes are called skills resumés. This resumé style shows how job seekers have developed skills. Job seekers show skills they gained through work, school, and other experiences.

Functional resumés can show job seekers' skills in many ways. They may show job seekers' abilities at the kind of work they seek. For example, job seekers may want to work in day care centers. They may list volunteer experience at children's summer camps on their resumés. Volunteers are people who work for free.

Functional resumés help job seekers who have little work experience at the type of job they seek. These job seekers still can show employers they are good workers. New graduates often use functional resumés. Job seekers who have worked at many different kinds of jobs also use this resumé style.

Functional resumés show how job seekers have gained important job skills.

Mike Carlson
577 Hills Road
Somerset, KY 42502
(000) 000-0000

Objective   To work as a police officer

**Work
History**
- Frankfort Police Department, Frankfort, KY
  911 Dispatcher, 1996-1998

- Kentucky State Reformatory, LaGrange, KY
  Security Guard, 1993-1996

- Henderson's Hardware Store, Louisville, KY
  Security Guard, 1990-1993

**Relevant
Skills**
- completed K-9 handler certification
  program, Southwest Kennels, May 1992
- completed emergency medical technician
  training, Columbia Hospital, December 1993
- attended traffic training seminar, Eastern
  Kentucky University, 1995

Awards
- received certificate for catching the
  most shoplifters from Henderson's
  Hardware Store, 1993
- received Good Citizenship Award, city of
  Somerset, 1995

Education
- Basic training certification, Kentucky
  Department of Criminal Justice, Eastern
  Kentucky University, Richmond, KY
  Completed July 1996

References available upon request.

Chapter 9

Combination Resumés

Job seekers also may use combination resumés. These resumés combine parts of chronological and functional resumés.

Combination resumés can show job seekers' work histories and skills. For example, job seekers may want to become schoolteachers. They can list their teaching jobs in chronological order. But these job seekers also may have good communication skills. They can describe their ability to speak and write.

Many job seekers use combination resumés. These resumés are flexible. They can be used to fit many different situations.

Some job seekers use combination resumés to make sure their resumés are complete. They want to include all information that will help them get jobs.

Job seekers can use combination resumés to show their work histories and skills.

Chapter 10

Electronic Resumés

Job seekers sometimes write electronic resumés. They place these resumés on the Internet. The Internet allows people to share information with others through computers. Job seekers can share their electronic resumés with a large number of employers.

Job seekers often put their electronic resumés in Internet databases. These computer databases store many electronic resumés. Some employers use the databases to find certain resumés easily. They use computers to scan the resumés. The computers look for key words. These important words match certain job positions that employers have available.

Job seekers must write electronic resumés differently from other resumé styles. Electronic resumés should only have words. They do not have underlining or other design features. Computers easily scan and read these simple resumés.

Employers use computers to find electronic resumés in Internet databases.

Chapter 11

Gaining Experience

Job seekers sometimes have very little information to include on their resumés. These job seekers may gain experience and skills to add to their resumés.

Many job seekers gain education to include on their resumés. For example, they may learn to speak another language. These job seekers may add this information to their education sections on resumés.

Some job seekers join groups related to their job interests. Many schools have groups that job seekers can join. Job seekers can include group names on their resumés. They make sure to include any leadership positions they had in these groups.

Some job seekers receive military training. These job seekers may learn many job skills. They can include information such as ranks, dates of service, and duties on their resumés.

Job seekers may gain military experience to add to their resumés.

Chapter 12

Keeping Resumés Current

Job seekers who receive jobs still keep their resumés current. They may want other jobs in the future.

Many job seekers gain experience as they work at jobs. They may join groups related to their job areas. They may take classes or workshops. Job seekers keep track of these experiences. They add dates, names, and other details about the experiences to their resumés.

The best way to prepare resumés may change over time. For example, a certain resumé style may become less popular with some employers. Job seekers may need to find current information about how to prepare resumés.

Job seekers with current resumés are ready for new opportunities. Current resumés can save time when people decide to seek different jobs.

Job seekers who receive jobs keep track of their experiences.

Words to Know

database (DAY-tuh-bayss)—a collection of information on a computer

employer (em-PLOI-uhr)—a person or company that hires and pays workers

Internet (IN-tur-net)—a system that allows people to share information with others through computers; job seekers put their resumés in databases on the Internet.

objective (uhb-JEK-tiv)—a job goal listed at the top of a resumé

reference (REF-uh-renss)—a person who can make statements about a job seeker's character and abilities

resumé (RE-zuh-may)—a written summary of a person's work history, education, awards, and other important experiences; job seekers write resumés to get job interviews.

To Learn More

Block, Jay A. and Michael Betrus. *101 Best Resumés.* New York: McGraw-Hill, 1997.

Potter, Ray. *Electronic Resumés That Get Jobs.* New York: Macmillan General Reference, 1996.

Schwartz, Stuart and Craig Conley. *Interviewing for a Job.* Looking at Work. Mankato, Minn.: Capstone High/Low Books, 1998.

Schwartz, Stuart and Craig Conley. *Setting Career Goals.* Life Skills. Mankato, Minn.: Capstone High/Low Books, 1998.

Useful Addresses

Human Resources Development Canada
140 Promenade du Portage, Phase IV
Hull, QC K1A 0J9
Canada

National Career Development Association
4700 Reed Road, Suite M
Columbus, OH 43220

U.S. Department of Labor
Office of Public Affairs
200 Constitution Avenue NW
Room S-1032
Washington, DC 20210

Internet Sites

America's Talent Bank

http://www.ajb.dni.us/html/atb_home.html

CanadaWorkInfoNet

http://www.workinfonet.ca/cwn

CareerMosaic

http://www.careermosaic.com/cm/crc

JobTrak

http://www.jobtrak.com

Index